How To Survive An « Urban » City

By
Ray Seest

FOREWORD

ARE YOU SURROUNDED BY THE « BLESSINGS » OF DIVERSITY? BUT CURSED WITH AN INFANTILE MIND THAT CANNOT CONNECT THE DOTS?

OF COURSE NOT, EVERYTHING THAT YOU SEE CAN BE EXPLAINED BY PLUNGING YOUR HEAD DEEPER IN THE SANDS OF VIBRANCY...HOWEVER, LET'S READ ON TO MAKE SURE YOU DON'T GET BUGGERED IN THE REAR WHILE PLUNGING YOUR HEAD DOWN BECAUSE WE REALLY WOULD NOT WANT TO LOSE YOUR SPECIAL LITTLE UNICORN SNOWFLAKE SELF NOW WOULD WE.

RAY SEEST'S TIPS ON « URBAN » PLACES

These tips will help you save yourself (and your family or « wuv ») from getting enriched with vibrant multiculturalism (often painfully, occasionally fatally).
Follow them, don't worry your little head about the why's if you feel like you need to run to your nearest safe-space and cry into a puppy because they shatter your idealistic world view with a healthy dose of reality.

And remember, reality, like your high school gym coach, does not give a shit about your feels.

So read on, intrepid and unique adventurer, this might save your worthless life so you can invite more diversity to make your life more difficult while earning brownie points in your social club. YAY!

It is even written in big font so you can happily and easily read it without having to tax your brain too much.

HOW TO IDENTIFY « VIBRANT! » NEIGHBORHOODS : COFFEE SHOPS

1. Does your national sugar-laden amazingly social justic-ey favorite coffee shop (which you wuvvvvv!!) have a lock on the bathroom door? What?! Travesty!
Congrats, you're in Vibrantopia

2. Does your plus-size barista having symbol of coffee love coffee-shop have the sugar, milk etc behind the counter?
Tch...tch...so inconvenient but guess what? You're gonna get grabbed by Vibrantopians!

3. Is there a noticeable lack of free Wi-Fi and sitting space? Are there multiple instructions on obvious good manners?
You have just entered....The Twilight Zone of Coffee shops, get out before you get a taste of authentic coffee beans in this Stabbucks.

HOW TO IDENTIFY « VIBRANT! » NEIGHBORHOODS : BURGER JOINTS

1. <u>Does your favorite carb-laden amazingly cheap and favorite burger joint (with processed magenta meat! Yum!) have a bathroom only for customers?</u>
   <u>Ruuude!</u>
   Congrats, you're in Vibrantopia

2. <u>Does the smell of fries and burgers which waft alluringly towards you mix with the unique scent of one or more home-challenged individuals who happen to be having an « engaging » conversation with the staff whenever you are there?</u>
   Ding, ding, ding…. Urban banana time!

3. <u>Do you feel like you are visiting an exotic foreign country and that too right here at your doorstep! No one else looks like you, and everyone is staring at you with let's just say aggressive interest.</u>
   <u>You're a Star!</u>
   And about to be enriched in 5 minutes unless you

remember that incredibly important meeting you have away from this shining gem of Urbantopia!

4. <u>Did you have to talk to the very nice lady at the counter with a very thick and unique accent and ask for ketchup, condiments etc.?</u>
<u>They just forgot to put them out in public right?</u>
You are in a temple of Urbantopia. Don't kneel in awe, you might get a steel-implant in your sides.

5. <u>Well what's this? You want to pay the cashier at a drive through but there seems to be a complicated payment system of some very thick windows with high-tech speakers to communicate with.</u>
<u>Wow! Technology!</u>
Grab your food and run before you get bombarded with affection, because you have reached a level which is Over 9000! of Vibrant Town!

6. <u>Welp! Where are the napkins! OMG how will you eat this amazingly delish but messy burger? And why is it that everytime you come here there are no napkins, and why does that female have 25 of them? Maybe you can ask her for one politely, she IS glaring</u>

<u>at you but that's just because she doesn't know how much you support her struggle!</u>
Yeah, before you make a move on a Jabba-the-napkin-hutt you could make another move, sideways, to the left...and out the door because you're gonna have that napkin thrust up your special place because hey guess what, you're in Diversityland! It's like Disneyland but with more stabbing and no food.

7. <u>Is the staff made up of people from such diverse backgrounds! They seem to be all from the SAME diverse background though...strange, oh well.</u>
<u>They're mean mugging you as well, they must have had a bad day poor things.</u>
Do you like having spit in your food? How about getting food enriched from the diverse flavor of ass-crack and pubic hair. And terrible service?
Oh you do? Stay by all means and tip them well, they really love you, you know. (Not Serious)

HOW TO IDENTIFY « VIBRANT! » NEIGHBORHOODS : MINI MARKET EDITION

1. <u>Whew! It's so hot, you're just gonna grab a cool refreshing drink from the freezer in this mini-market, but hold on…the freezer seems to be located far away from the door.
Treasure hunt!</u>
Calm down lampedusa, this one is subtle, the farther away the freezer with bottles in ice are from the door, the greater the degree of vibrancy in this place you call charming and « ethnic"

2. <u>There's no open freezer with bottles at all, w-what? Will you actually have to walk down to the freezers and grab a couple, blaah</u>
Do yourself a favour, grab the door handle and exit stage left before you get grabbed by your love handles because guess what, Vibrant!

3. <u>The very friendly cashier seems grumpy and is behind some sort of weird thick glass and is locked in behind a door as well, poor guy, it's like your cubicle, the struggle is real, yo!</u>

How touching, you know what else is touching, the guy behind the cash register has been « Diversitied! » so many times that the glass you see is bulletproof and he is probably packing heat because his struggle is real…against getting shot, because you are in such a dynamic! vibrant! place. Get. Out.

4. <u>Oh look! Some « youth » hanging out outside the place, this must be a social spot for them. How lively!</u>

Very social, the fact that most of them are mean mugging you and wearing suspiciously 90s baggy clothing means you might shortly get a case of lead-poisoning or if you're a pretty little snowflake, you might get an attack of surprise-penis! Because your lost little lamb is in the middle of an Urban Block Party yo.
Turn around, get in your hoopty (vibrant name for car!) and get out of there.

HOW TO IDENTIFY « VIBRANT! » NEIGHBORHOODS : GAS STATIONS

1. Blink! Blink! oh, in your amazing drive through the richness and diversity of your city you are out of gas, hey there's a gas station, let's pop in real quick, but why is it poorly lit. And why is that group of men hanging around without a car? Are they lost? Should i give them directions?

How kind of you! They're not lost, they are looking to borrow some money from kind gentle unique supportive diversity-loving unicorns like you, and by borrow i mean permanently borrow, they might even leave a mark or ten of their appreciation on you while borrowing this money. And wave a funny looking thing that goes bang at you while doing it.

Don't stop little red retarded hood, go to a better gas station, or if you have to, get out, pretend talk loudly on your cellphone and get a gallon of gas and run.

2. Your card won't work, you walk in to pay the cashier but again are confused by the thick-glass, also there seem to be a lot of gentle giants with

saggy pants walking around this tiny store, wow some of them are loud, how refreshing from the quietness of your neighborhood.
Two things are gonna happen, the store is gonna get enriched in about 2 minutes and by enriched we mean, the gentle giants are gonna be richer the store is gonna be poorer. The other thing that's gonna happen is that your pretty little self is gonna get catcalled and then pussy-whipped and enriched by Urban Youth.
LEAVE. NOW.

3. This mini-mart has bars on the windows. What great security. Although they could do with a little more window cleaner, it looks a little too baroque.
Yes, the bars are there for a reason, there have been random cultural enrichments of this establishment in the past when it had no bars, the bars keep diversity out. You need to get out. FAST.

HOW TO IDENTIFY « VIBRANT! » NEIGHBORHOODS : MISC

1. <u>Why are there no farmers markets here? Where is the take a penny leave a penny stand? Why is there no farm fresh, take what you want and drop money in the jar stand?</u>
Welcome to the blessings of Urban Town, you must be new here, if you think those things can work here i've got a bridge in Brooklyn to sell you, call me!

2. <u>Boy, there sure are a lot of Pawn Shops and Check Cashing places here, this must be a centre of finance!</u>
Unless your definition of finance is robbing a bank while shooting a child, you are in a very diverse neighborhood homie, keep driving.

3. <u>Someone got shot! And by the authorities no less, oh look here's a picture of him as a 9 year old. The horror! Wait, wasn't he 15-17? Why didn't they put the selfie of him holding hilarious gang-signs and guns up?</u>
You are in a sorrowful procession in a vibrant

neighbourhood, please leave or there will be two funerals here today pumpkin.

4. <u>oooh! So many cars that look like they are from my favorite cartoon shows! And parked on both sides of the street! Such creativity , let me go and compliment them!</u>
Keep your compliment in your pants unless you want to be pistol-whipped for not looking diverse enough, hey, it's not your fault you were born that way, they are just misunderstood and are taking your car apart and breaking your legs due to the discrimination they've suffer....(you blackout).

5. <u>oh look! a road named after Martin Luther King Jr, Or even Washington Drive! Or Cesar Chavez! Or (Insert Vibrant Civil Wrongs Leader here) How historical?</u>
Well done cupcake, you noticed the warning signs, you are now entering a magical land of bad roads, overflowing trash, beat up cars, random roving gangs of « youth » and generally a sense of being in an exotic (though smelly) third world paradise. Proceed and you shall reap the

rewards of being a retard.

6. <u>Well this neighborhood seems a little too vibrant but this restaurant piping Mozart seems to be a gem from your small town.</u>

Little known fact, Diversity in music usually caters to the definition of Diverse. Classical music repels diversity, is classical music racist? Well, at least it allows you to drink your coffee in peace before going out to find out that your car is missing all four tires and come to think of it, that hole in the windshield wasn't there when you came in.

7. <u>Waterpark time! Hmm, this waterpark seems to be really busy right now, and oops you're the only one who doesn't have black hair, you're so lame LOL!</u>

This waterpark is a level 5 toxic dump where you will be manhandled by Diversity and have your body be critically examined by strange people, intimately. But hey if you like getting roughed up and forced into enrichment, go in by all means.

The water's fine (although kinda dirty and smells funky, is your nose racist?)

8. <u>Party time! Night time! Welp, why are there gangs</u>

<u>of Urban Youth out tonight? Maybe there is a special Vibrant food festival in town?</u>
Yes, there is a food festival for Vibrance! in town and the main course is you, your great dress and dapper threads are going to attract a lot of attention from Diversity and you might find yourself drugged and deprived of them and your right-to-not-get-assaulted (in more ways than one) Check where you are partying, and then dump the friends who suggested it.
Alternatively you could become famous!
Yes!
Really!
As a crime statistic.
Idiot.

8. <u>It's a great day out! Let's go out for a walk or ride our bike...(16 hours later) Hello? What's this? Where am I? And why is there a surprise penis in my mouth/ass?</u>
You took a wild ride on the Vibrant Side! of town, congrats you just got drugged and enriched by that gentle giant (Or just a group of smelly trolls) whose name rhymes with abc-onte, xyz-jamaal and stradivarious.

Must have been the racism in you, you didn't want to look racist when that strange person approached and then 3 more did. And it would have been rude to decline that drink, what would you have said, you were a recovering alcoholic?
Well, guess you'll just have to get new teeth and rest at home for a few years with your torn asshole.
It's all good. They didn't do nuffin.

9. <u>This restaurant has a lot of unhappy customers/staff? The struggle of diversity is real.</u>
<u>We must help them. Why did that person suddenly throw a chair?</u>
Ok, count to 1 in your head, then run. All these colorful people you are surrounded by feeling all holy and lovey-dovey about openness and acceptance are about to start a mini-party (Fun!...??) No, not that kind of party, the kind of party where they are gonna destroy stuff, punch people and you will end up with either a black eye or a dick in your ass (Or multiple!)
Again.
What were you thinking coming to a place like this?
To show appreciation for your new world?
You're gonna get appreciated right back..to death... real soon.

EPILOGUE

These handy hints are gathered from around the world and billions of experiences where « Diversity! », « Vibrancy! » and « Urban! » mean the same, look pretty similar and behave the same.

It's short, it's easy and you can easily prove it if you would like your head blown off.

If the contents of this book made your vagina hurt, please go ahead and try to do the opposite of what is suggested, and don't report back with the results, as we will just be sitting here laughing at you.

If you feel guilty about the truth in this book, well, that's what cupcakes are for fatass.

Or you could go online and search for the truth of these, then join a gym and lose some weight and open your eyes and close your gaping ass so you are not unduly and inadvertently enriched by Diversitah!

Still To Come......

1.   Snowflake : A Journey Against Reality
(An Epic Adventure! The Quest For Retardation By A Mentally ill girl/boy-man.)

5 Pages For Your Angsty Thoughts

4 Pages For Your Angsty Thoughts

3 Pages For Your Angsty Thoughts

2 Pages For Your Angsty Thoughts

Guess What?

Chicken Butt.

If you're a pretty girl (And no, fat isn't pretty) show your appreciation

Send Noodz

Printed in Great Britain
by Amazon